W9-CQU-019

Massimo Lucchesi

COACHING THE
3-4-3

Library of Congress Cataloging - in - Publication Data

by Lucchesi, Massimo
  Coaching the 3-4-3

ISBN No. 1-890946-43-5
Library of Congress Catalog Number 00-101764
Copyright © April 2000

Originally printed in Italy - 1999 by Edizioni Nuova Prhomos Via O.
Bettacchini. Translated by Sestiltio Polimanti

All rights reserved. Except for use in a review. The reproduction of uti-
lization of this book in any form or by any electronic, mechanical, or
other means, now known or hereafter invented, including xerography,
photocopying, and recording, and in any information storage and
retrieval system, is forbidden without written permission of the pub-
lisher.

Art Direction/Book Layout
Kimberly N. Bender

Editing and Proofing
Bryan R. Beaver

Printed by
DATA REPRODUCTIONS

Cover Photograph
EMPICS

REEDSWAIN INC
612 Pughtown Road • Spring City • Pennsylvania 19475
1-800-331-5191• www.reedswain.com

To my wife Stefania and to my children

This book would never have been published without the support of my parents, Liliana and Giuliano.

I would also like to give special recognition to the following clubs: Nuove Leve Massarosa, U.S. Bozzano and C.G.C. Viareggio. Thanks to them I have been able to coach and to gain important professional experience. Special thanks also to Mr. Michelotti and Mr. Del Bucchia (Nuove Leve), Mr. Luporini and Mr. Evangelisti (Bozzano), Mr. D'Angelo and Mr. Barsanti (C.G.C. Viareggio). They have always been helpful to me and have shown their faith in me. I have shared with them joys and disappointments.

Finally, many thanks to all the players I have coached. Their involvement, patience and sacrifices have been instrumental in my improvement as a coach.

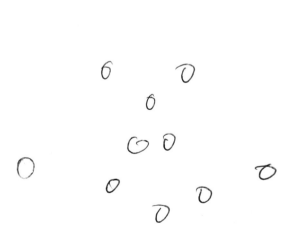

Massimo Lucchesi

COACHING THE
3-4-3

Published by
REEDSWAIN INC

Heide M

Peter

Heide S

Vicki ?

Alex   Munson
         Simmons
Kailee   Ferran   Laura
Katie   Lauren   Zoe   Holly

Legend

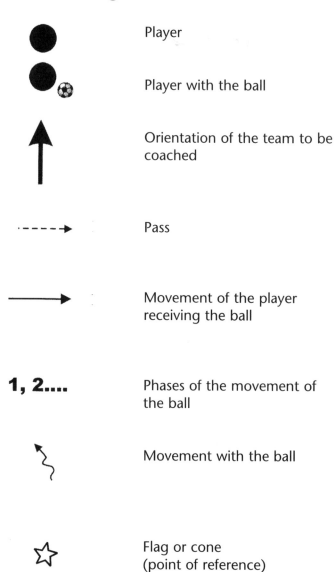

Player

Player with the ball

Orientation of the team to be coached

Pass

Movement of the player receiving the ball

1, 2....

Phases of the movement of the ball

Movement with the ball

Flag or cone
(point of reference)

1 1 Goalkeeper

2 2 Right side back

3 3 Left side back

4 4 Left center midfielder

5 5 Central back

6 6 Right center back

7 7 Right wing

8 8 Left side midfielder

9 Center forward

10 Right side midfielder

11 Left wing

All the following exercises, tactical examples, situations and schemes can of course be applied and used in a mirror-like way in the part of the field opposite to the one shown in the diagrams.

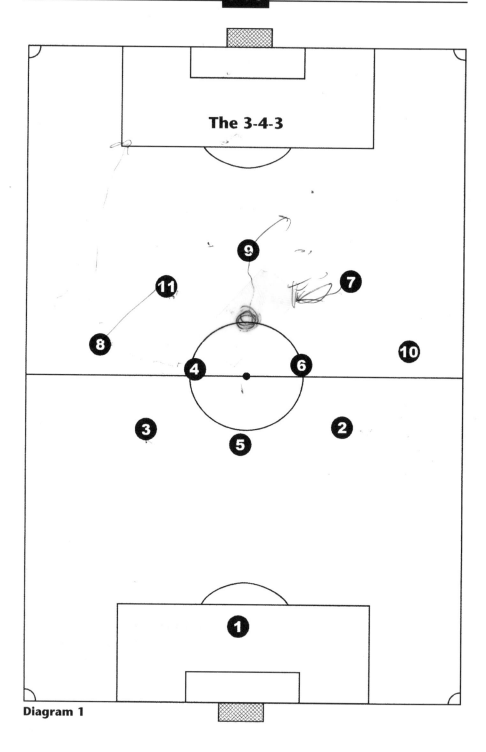

The 3-4-3

Diagram 1

CHAPTER ONE

DESCRIPTION OF THE 3-4-3 PATTERN OF PLAY

In addition to the goalkeeper, the 3-4-3 alignment provides for three backs, four midfielders and three forwards.

The three forwards are positioned in a triangle-like arrangement: the top vertex of this triangle corresponds to the position of the center-forward, while the two corners of the triangle are the positions on the wings.

Analysis of the roles of the players

The three-player defense is made up of a central back and two side backs.

Usually, in the 3-4-3 the defense plays and shifts according to the mechanisms of zone play, but sometimes it may be better for the central back to shift the marking while the side back individually marks the opposing forward. The choice depends on the coach's philosophy and on the skills of his players.

Central back: on defense, he must be good at shifting the marking and at tackling the opponent with the ball.

On offense, he must show tactical knowledge and be quick and accurate when he passes the ball. He must make himself available for possible back passes from his teammates and have good kicking skills in order to be able to make long passes to the center-forward when appropriate.

Therefore, a player with very good technical and tactical skills should be chosen for this position.

Side back: he must be good at individual marking and at anticipating the opponent. On offense, he must make himself available on the wings, so he needs to have remarkable physical and athletic skills.

The midfield is made up of four players arranged along the same line: two center midfielders and two side midfielders.

Center midfielder: he must be good at play-making and at developing deep play. At least one of the two center midfielders must have remarkable defending skills, be good at applying pressure and at winning the ball.

Side midfielder: he must be a flexible player. He must cover the whole wing, therefore he needs to have good athletic and technical skills, and also tactical vision. On defense, he must become the fourth defender. On offense, he must support the action by making himself available to carry out crossing passes or to shoot from far out.

The attack is made up of three forwards: the center forward and the wings.
Wing: on offense, his effectiveness depends on his ability to carry out deep cut-ins and diagonal cut-ins towards the center. Besides, he must make himself available for wall passes in combination with the center-forward. He must possess good shooting skills and, when he has the ball, he must be able to dribble it past the opponent and make penetrating passes to his teammates. On defense, he is required to play as a fourth midfielder on the weak side of the field.

Center-forward: he is typically the "target player" - good at receiving and keeping the ball. He must make himself available for wall passes enabling the wing to penetrate and must attack deeply at the right time. He needs to have very good shooting and dribbling skills.

3 - 3 - 3 - 1

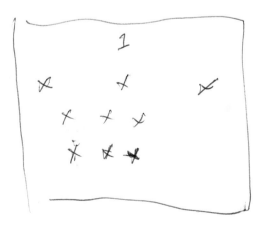

CHAPTER Two
OFFENSIVE SCHEMES

Main options according to each player's role in the "building-up" phase

• **Central back.**
He can pass the ball either to a side back (by a sideways pass) or to a center midfielder (by a diagonal pass). When possible, he should make a deep pass to the center-forward or to a wing.

• **Side back.**
He can make a back pass to the central back, but, when possible, a pass to the wing is preferable. Other options are a pass to a side or a center midfielder.

• **Side midfielder.**
He can pass the ball to a back or to the nearby midfielder. The best solution is a pass to the center-forward.

• **Center midfielder.**
He should vary the play through passes to the wings and to the center-forward.

Main options according to the player's role in the "final touch phase"

• **Center midfielder.**
He needs to be particularly good at making deep passes to the forwards.

• **Side midfielder.**
He needs to be good at overlapping the wing or at penetrating along the wing to make crossing passes. He can also make long passes to the center-forward.

• **Wing.**
He must be good at making penetrating passes to the center-forward, to the other wing cutting in, and to the overlapping side midfielder.

• **Center-forward.**
He must create space with his movement and with his wall passes, in order to enable his teammates, especially the wings, to penetrate.

Main options according to each player's role in the "shooting phase"

- **Center midfielder.**

He can either shoot from far out or he can penetrate without the ball in order to be in a position to receive a wall pass or a penetrating pass, and then shoot.

- **Side midfielder.**

He rarely shoots from far out. He enters the penalty area when the ball is crossed from the end of the field to get into a position to shoot.

- **Wing.**

He must be good at shooting from far out, and also at making the most of cut-ins, wall passes, crosses, combinations and dribbling to get into a position to shoot.

- **Center-forward.**

He must make the most of crossing and penetrating passes and "attack" the bouncing ball in order to shoot. He must be good at shooting from far out and, if needed, dribbling the ball past the opponent.

Building up play

The objective of the "building up" phase is to take the ball forward, towards the opposing goal, and to set up a shooting situation.
The building up phase can be accomplished by a long pass, a diagonal pass, or a deep pass with a followed-up back pass.
Let's consider now some examples of building up play with the 3-4-3 pattern.

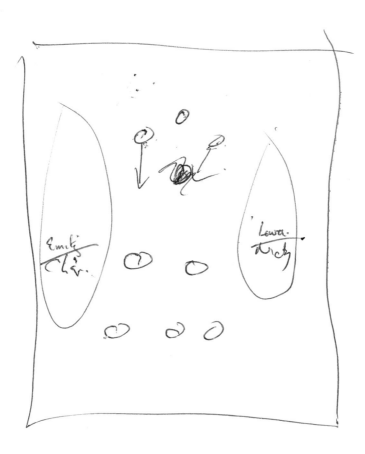

Building up play with a long pass

In diagram 2, central back 5 makes a long pass to center-forward 9, who can then either make a pass to wing 7 or to a penetrating midfielder.

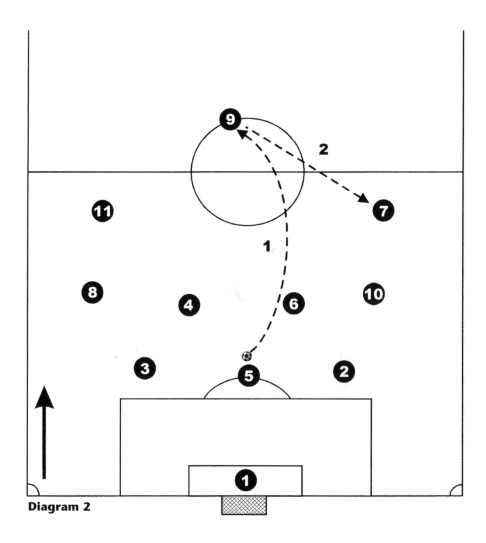

Diagram 2

Diagram 3 shows a scheme similar to the one in diagram 2. The only difference is that the long pass is carried out by a side back (player 2).

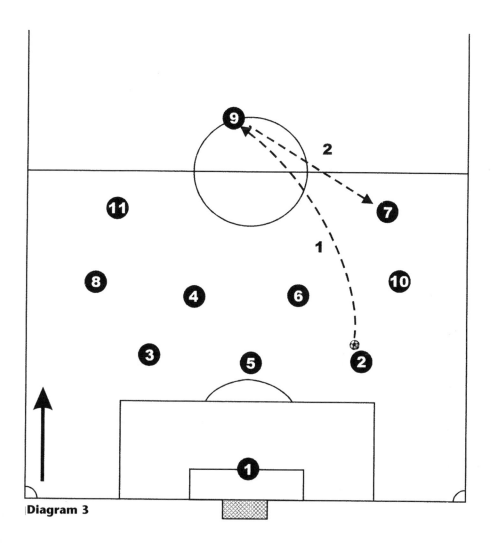

Diagram 3

Building up play with a diagonal pass

Central back 5 passes the ball to side back 2, who passes to side midfielder 10. Side midfielder 10 passes to center midfielder 6, who passes it to 4 who carries out an "encompassing movement". Center midfielder 4 makes a diagonal pass to wing 11, who can start the "final touch" phase.

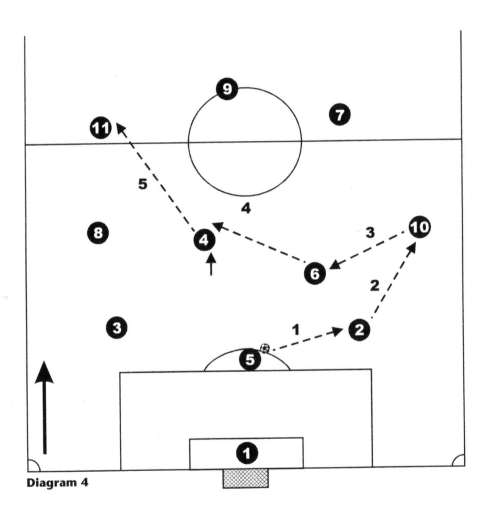

Diagram 4

Diagram 5 shows a scheme similar to the one in diagram 4. The only difference is that right side center midfielder 6 immediately makes a diagonal pass to wing 11, instead of passing the ball to the other center midfielder.

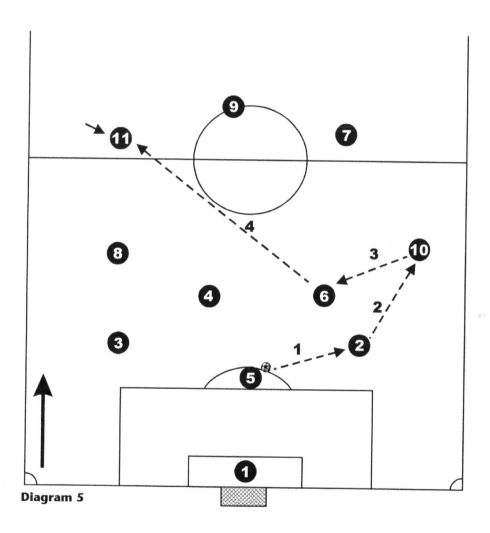

Diagram 5

Building up play with a deep pass and a subsequent back pass

Central back 5 passes the ball to center midfielder 6 who makes a back pass to side back 2. Side back 2 makes a deep pass to wing 7, who makes a back pass to side midfielder 10. Side midfielder 10 passes to center-forward 9 who makes a back pass to center midfielder 4, who can then penetrate or make a deep pass (see diagram 6).

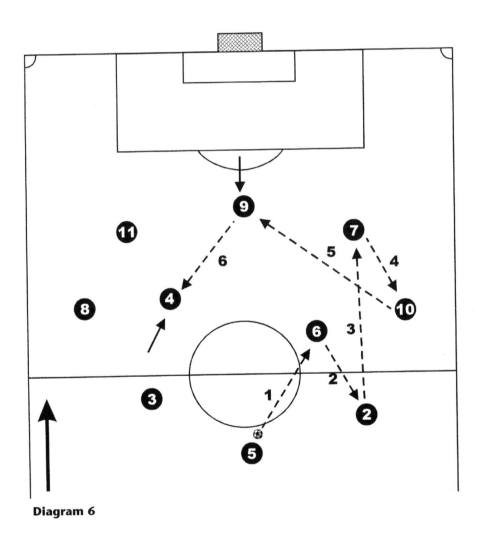

Diagram 6

In diagram 7, side back 2 passes to center midfielder 6, who makes a back pass to central back 5. Central back 5 makes a deep pass to center-forward 9, who can then make a back pass to left side center midfielder 4.

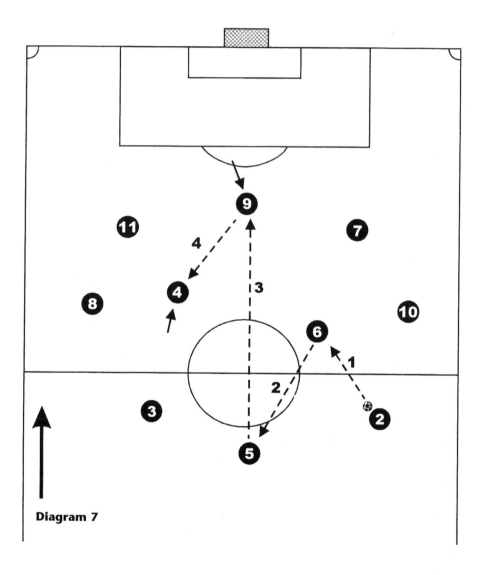

Diagram 7

In diagram 8, central back 5 receives a back pass from midfielder 6 and then makes a deep pass to wing 11, who can then make a back pass to nearby midfielder 4.

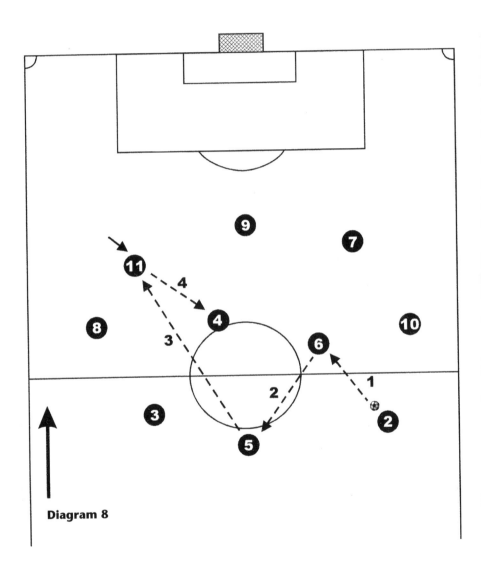

Diagram 8

In diagram 9, wing 11 makes a back pass to side midfielder 8 (instead of center midfielder 4). Side midfielder 8 makes a deep pass to center-forward 9, who can then make a back pass to center midfielder 4.

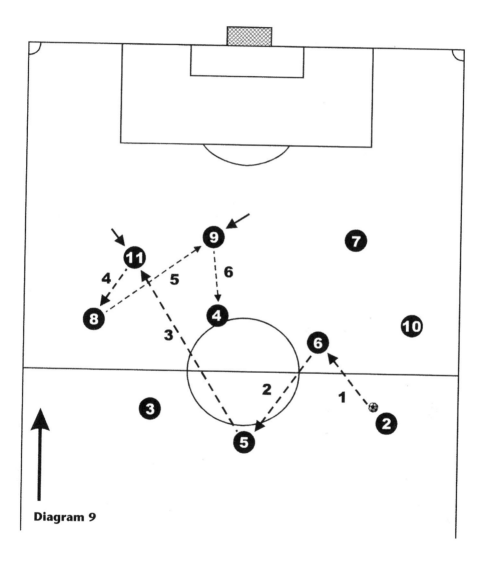

Diagram 9

In diagram 10, the action develops in the same way as in diagram 9. The only difference is that center-forward 9 makes a pass to wing 11, not to a midfielder.

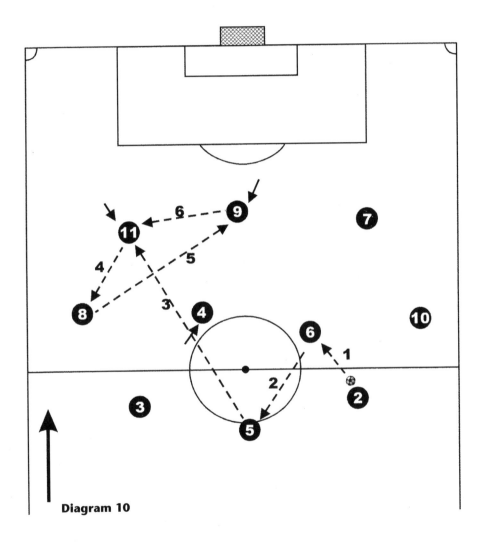

Diagram 10

Final touches

Final touches enable a player to unmark himself and shoot. Let's consider cut-ins, wall passes, combinations, overlappings and crosses in the 3-4-3 pattern.

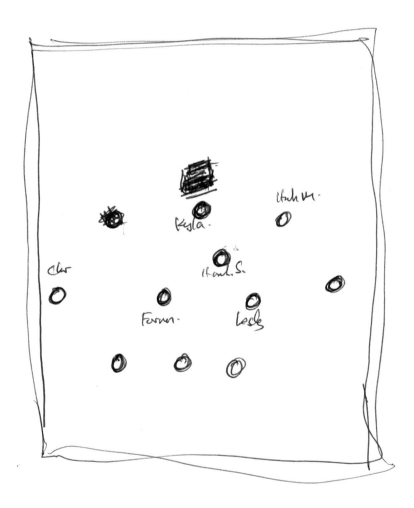

Cut-ins

Cut-in by the wing, assisted by the center midfielder (diagram 11)
When building up play with a deep pass followed up by a back pass, the center midfielder (player 6 here) makes a deep pass to the nearby wing (7) after receiving the ball.

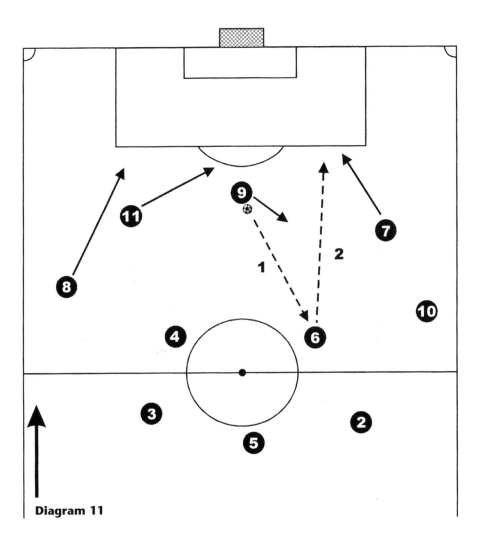

Diagram 11

Cut-in by the center-forward, assisted by the center midfielder (diagram 12)

This scheme differs from the previous one as the center-forward penetrates deeply while the nearby wing comes towards midfielder 6.

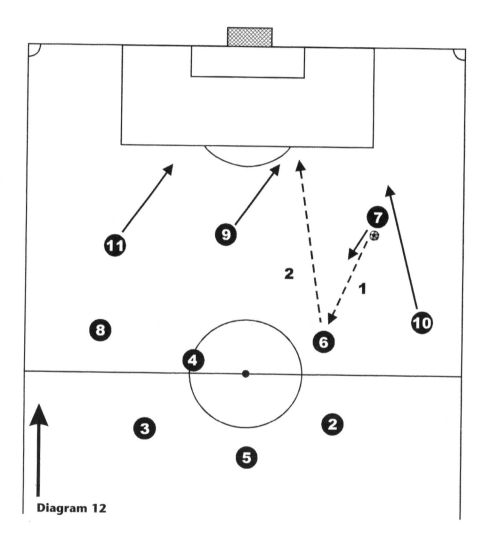

Diagram 12

Deep penetration by the center-forward, assisted by the center midfielder (diagram 13)

Unlike the previous scheme, the center-forward penetrates deeply with a wide movement.

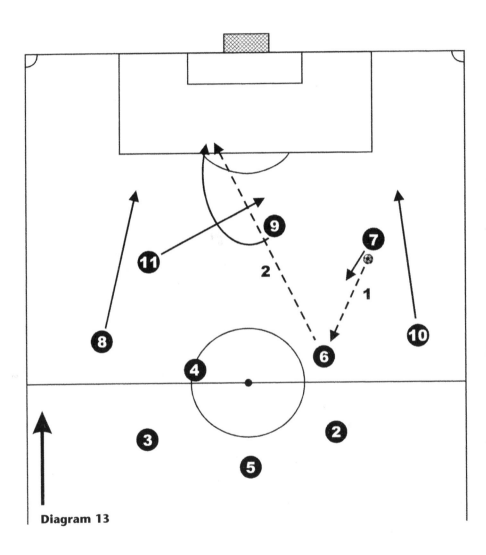

Diagram 13

Cut-in by the far wing, assisted by the center midfielder (diagram 14)

Center midfielder 6 makes a deep pass to far wing 11, who cuts in towards the goal. The center-forward carries out the same movement as in diagram 12, while wing 7 moves towards him for a possible combination and in to support the penetration by side midfielder 10.

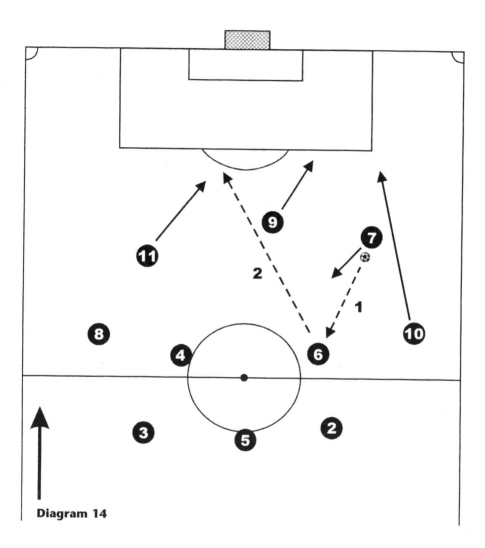

Diagram 14

Cut-in by the side midfielder, assisted by the center midfielder (diagram 16)

This exercise is similar to the previous one, but this time center midfielder 6 makes a deep pass to side midfielder 10, who has carried out a cut-in from behind.

The cut-in by midfielder 10 is supported by the movement of wing 7, who creates space.

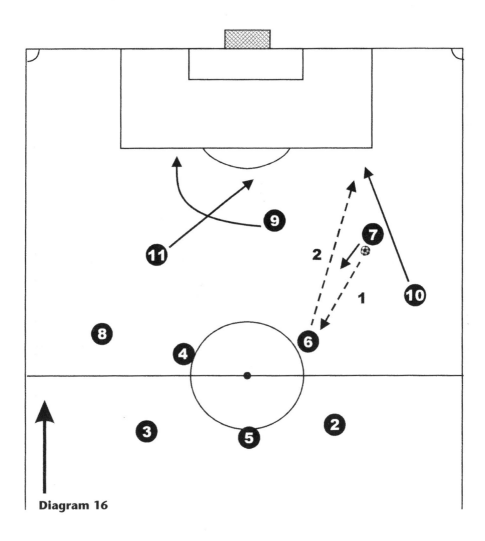

Diagram 16

Cut-in by the center midfielder, assisted by the other center midfielder (diagram 17)

Center midfielder 4 cuts in from behind, assisted by center midfielder 6. The movements of wing 11 and center-forward 9 are fundamental to creating space for the penetration by midfielder 4.

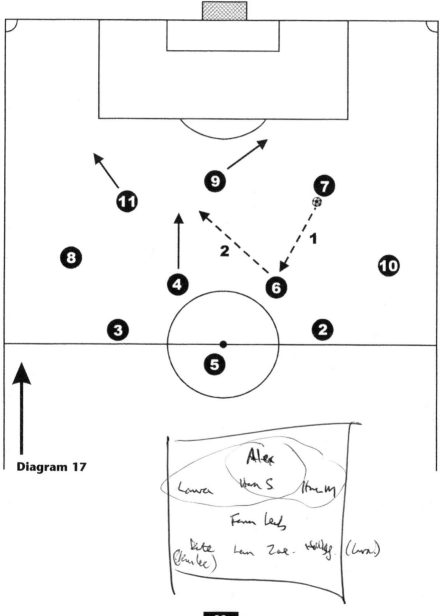

Diagram 17

Cut-in by the far wing, assisted by the side midfielder (diagram 18)

Side midfielder 10 makes a pass to far wing 11 who cuts in deeply. The movements of wing 7 and center-forward 9 are fundamental to creating space for the penetration by wing 11.

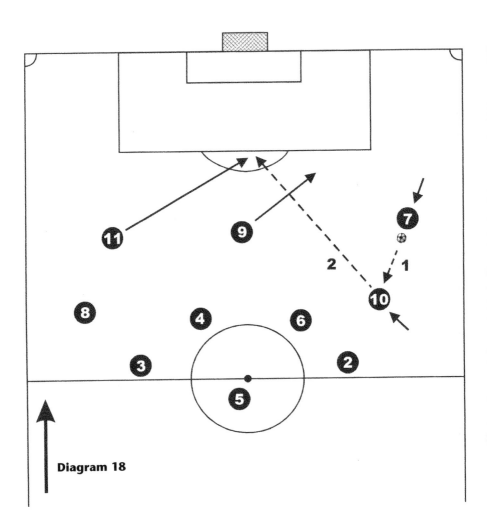

Diagram 18

Cut-in by the center-forward, assisted by the side midfielder (diagram 19)

This scheme is similar to the previous one, but side midfielder 10 makes a pass to center-forward 9.

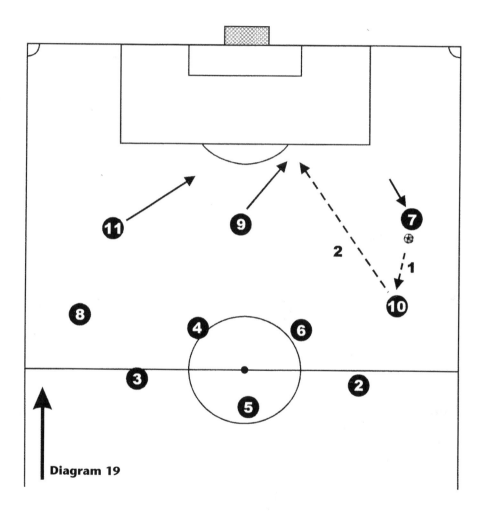

Diagram 19

Cut-in by the center-forward, assisted by the wing (diagram 20)
The final touch is carried out by wing 7. Wing 7 receives the ball from
midfielder 4 (he could also receive it from a back) and, after dribbling
it forward to the inside of the field, makes a pass to center-forward 9
who cuts in deeply.

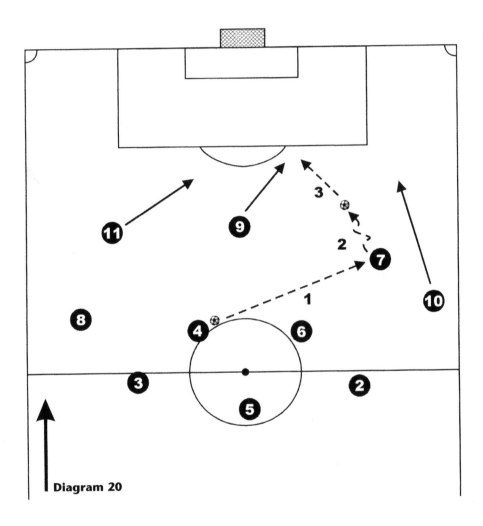

Diagram 20

Cut-in by the opposite wing, assisted by the other wing (diagram 21)

In this scheme, center-forward 9 and wing 11 carry out a criss-crossing movement. After receiving the ball from midfielder 4 (he could also receive it from a back), wing 7 makes a deep pass to 11, who cuts in.

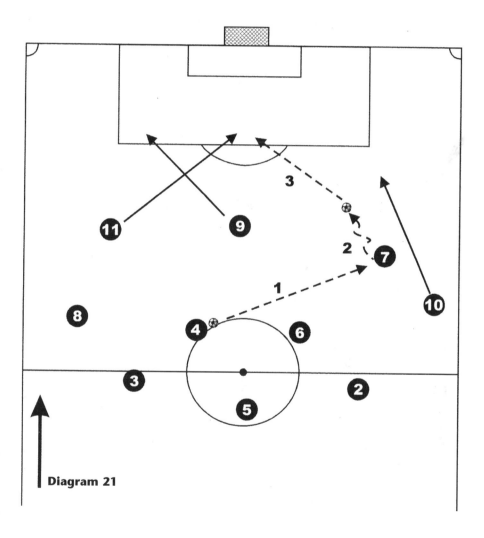

Diagram 21

Cut-in by the center-forward, assisted by the wing (diagram 22)

This scheme is similar to the previous one, but this time wing 7 receives the ball from 2 (he could also receive it from a center midfielder) and center-forward 9 unmarks himself with a wide movement.

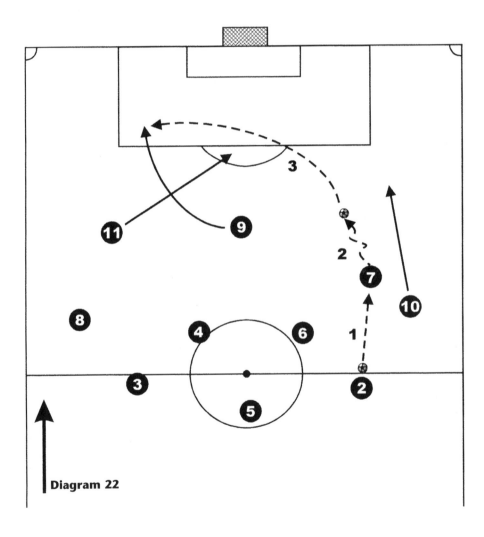

Diagram 22

Wall passes

Wall pass by the center-forward for the wing's cut-in (diagram 23)
Center midfielder 6 makes a deep pass to center-forward 9 who, instead of shooting, makes a wall pass to support wing 7's penetration.

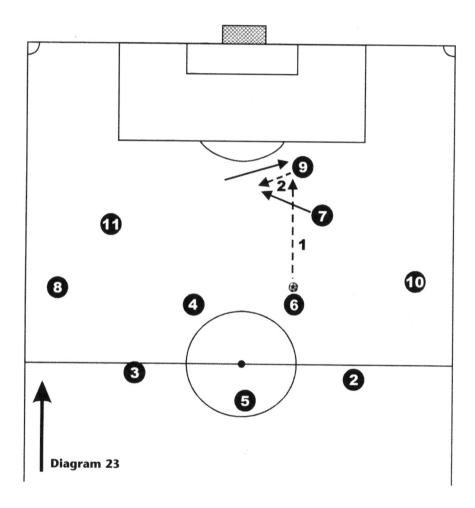

Diagram 23

Wall pass by the center-forward for the wing's cut-in (diagram 24)
This scheme is similar to the previous one. The only difference is that center-forward 9 receives the ball from side midfielder 10.

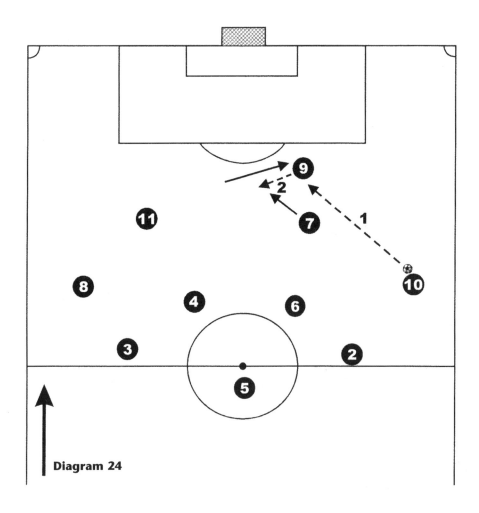

Diagram 24

Wall pass by the center-forward for the wing's penetration (diagram 25)

Instead of receiving a deep pass, center-forward 9 comes towards the pass made by side midfielder 10 and makes a wall pass to support wing 7's penetration.

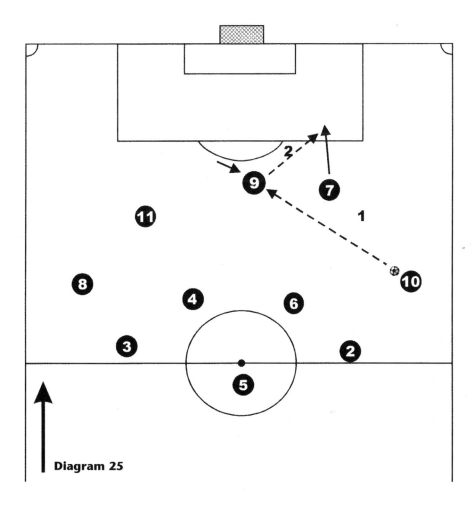

Diagram 25

Wall pass by the center-forward for the center midfielder's penetration (diagram 26)

Side midfielder 10 passes to center-forward 9, who comes towards the ball and then makes a wall pass to support the center midfielder's penetration.

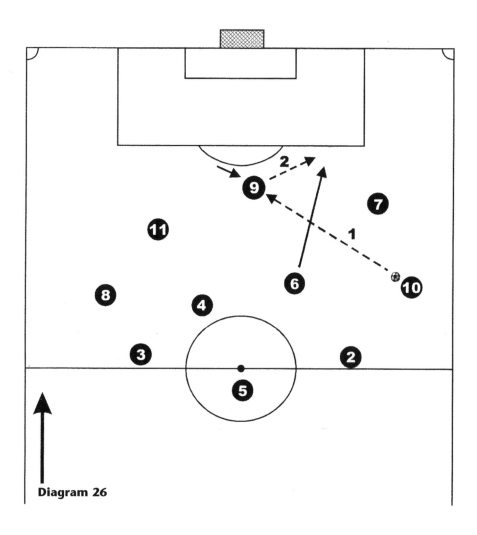

Diagram 26

Wall pass by the wing for the center midfielder's penetration (diagram 27)

Center midfielder 6 passes the ball to wing 11, who comes towards the ball and by a wall pass supports the penetration of center midfielder 4. This penetration is made possible by the movement of center-forward 9, who moves to the side in order to create space.

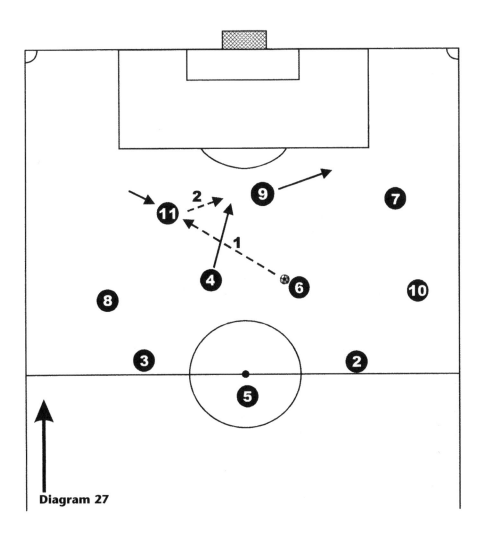

Diagram 27

Wall pass by the wing for the side midfielder's penetration (diagram 28)
Side back 2 makes a deep pass to wing 7, who makes a wall pass for side midfielder 10's penetration. If the side midfielder is too far from the goal to shoot, he can opt for a final touch to the center-forward or to the wing on the other side, as shown in diagrams 18, 19 and 32.

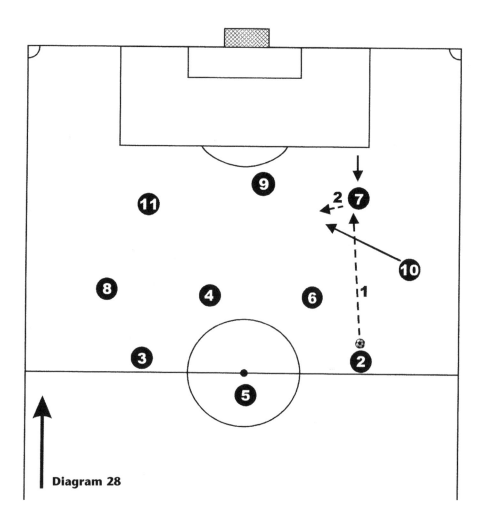

Diagram 28

Combinations

"Pass and follow": from the side midfielder to the wing (diagram 29)

Side midfielder 10 passes to wing 7 and moves forward to receive the return pass.

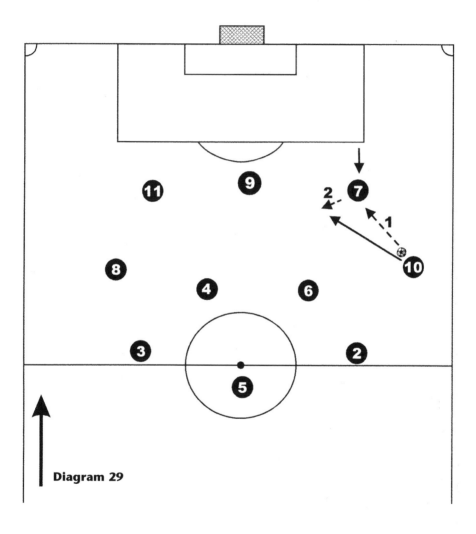

Diagram 29

"Pass and go": from the wing to the center-forward (diagram 30)
Wing 7 makes a one-two pass with the center-forward.

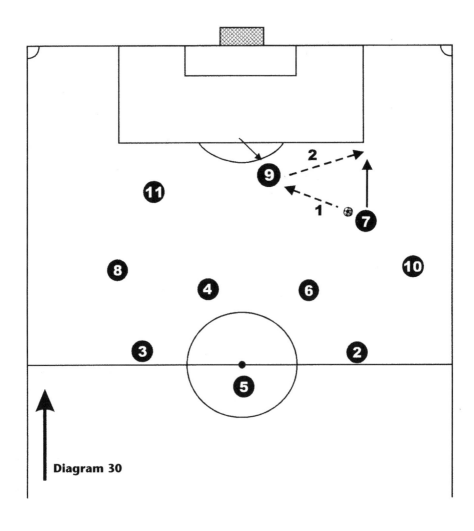

Diagram 30

"Pass and go": from the center midfielder to the center-forward (diagram 31)

Center midfielder 4 makes a one-two pass with the center-forward.

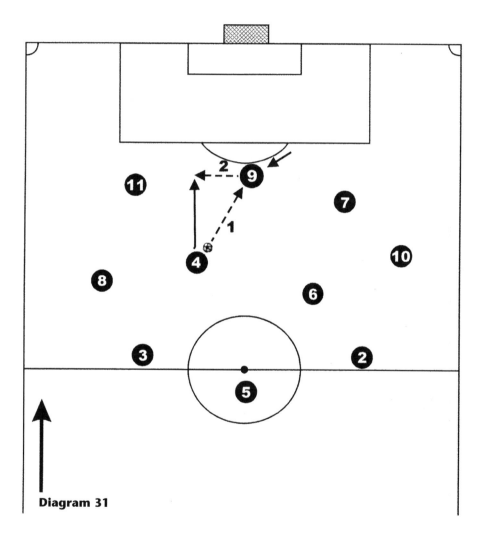

Diagram 31

Dummy movement by the center-forward to favor the wing (diagram 32)

When side midfielder 10 makes the pass, center-forward 9 makes a dummy movement to favor wing 11's penetration.

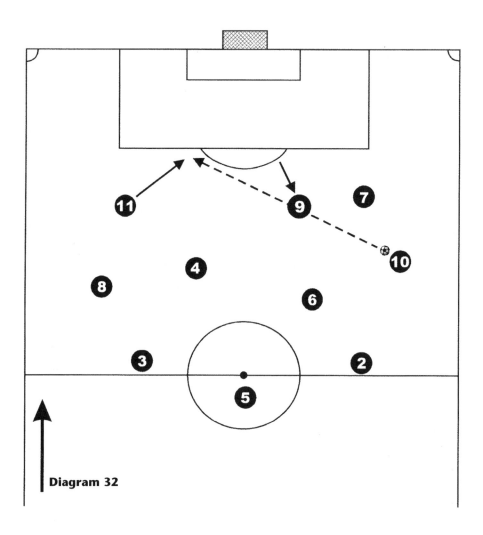

Diagram 32

Dummy movement by the wing to favor the side midfielder (diagram 33)

Center midfielder 6 makes a pass to wing 7, who comes towards the ball and carries out a dummy movement to support the penetration of side midfielder 10.

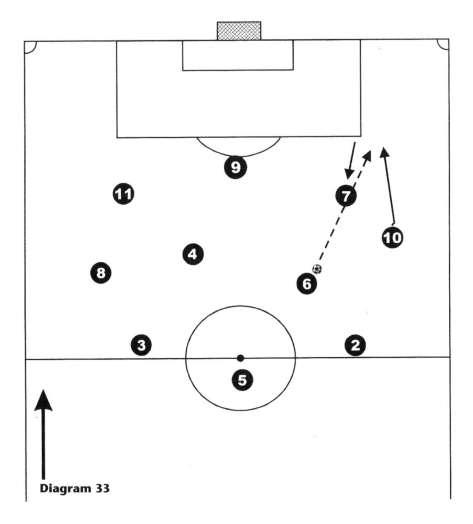

Diagram 33

Dummy movement by the wing to favor the side midfielder (diagram 34)
Center midfielder 6 makes a pass to wing 11, who comes towards the ball and carries out a dummy movement to support the penetration of side midfielder 8.

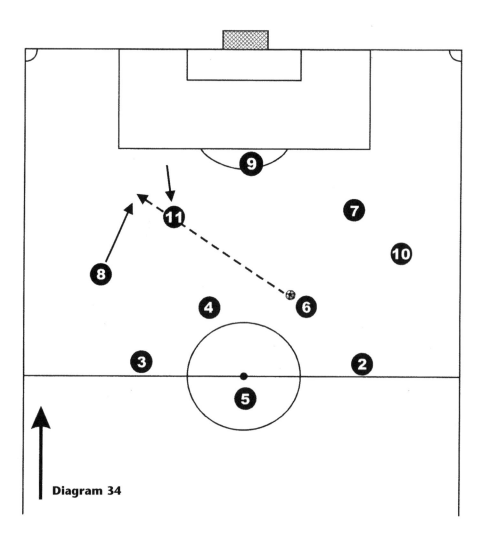

Diagram 34

Dummy movement + "pass and go": center-forward and wing (diagram 35)
This movement is the natural development of the action shown in diagram 32. When side midfielder 10 makes the pass, center-forward 9 first carries out a dummy movement to support wing 11, then moves forward to receive the return pass from 11.

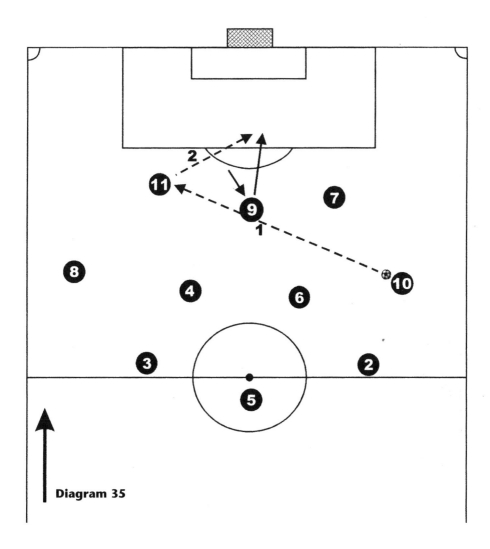

Diagram 35

Overlapping

The wing favoring the side midfielder (diagram 36)

From player 7's position, a wing usually makes a deep pass to the forwards or carries out a combination with them. Diagram 36 shows an alternative where wing 7 supports the penetration by side midfielder 10 who makes an overlapping movement.

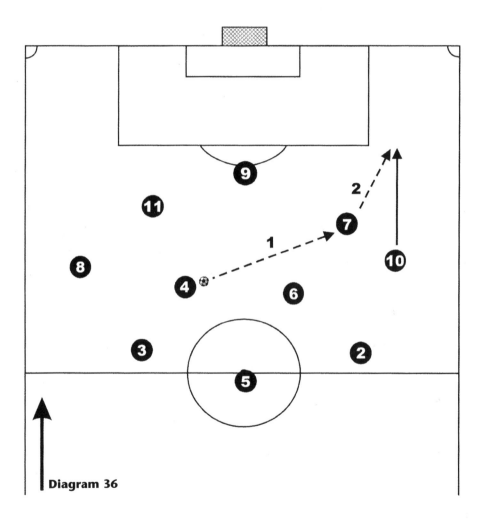

Diagram 36

Crosses

Position and movements of the receivers in the penalty area (diagram 37)

At least two forwards must be ready in the penalty area to cover the near post and the central zone.

The far post zone and the zone outside the penalty area must be covered by a side midfielder and a center midfielder.

The player making the crossing pass must have a supporting player behind him, ready to receive a possible back pass.

Diagram 37

Pass from the center midfielder to the wing (diagram 38)

Center midfielder 6 makes a deep pass to wing 7, who can cross.

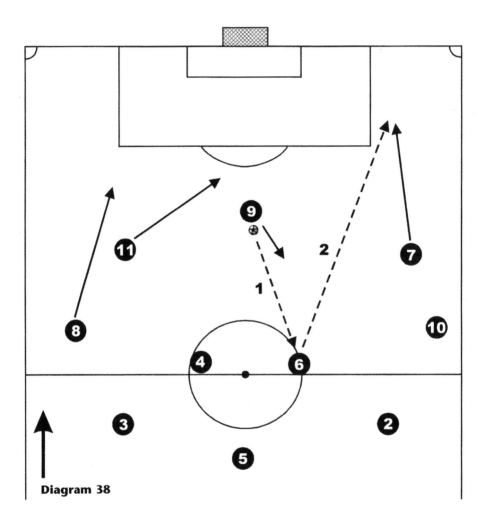

Diagram 38

Pass from the center midfielder to the side midfielder (diagram 39)

Side midfielder 10 makes a deep cut-in and can receive the ball because of the movement of wing 7 who has created space by cutting towards the center. Side midfielder 10 can then cross.

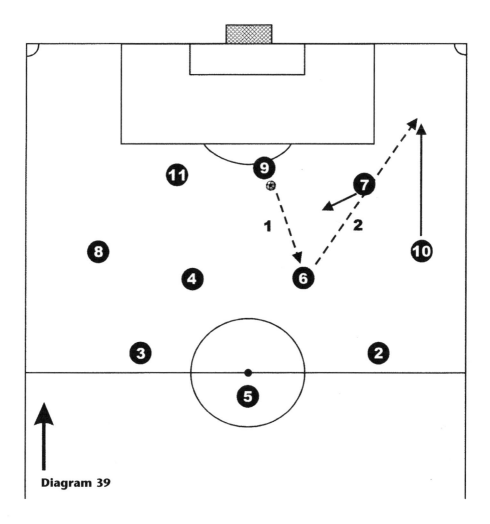

Diagram 39

Pass from the center-forward, who is cutting in, to the wing (diagram 40)
In this case, side midfielder 10 makes a deep pass to center-forward 9, who makes a wall pass to penetrating wing 7. Wing 7 moves forward to the end of the field and crosses.

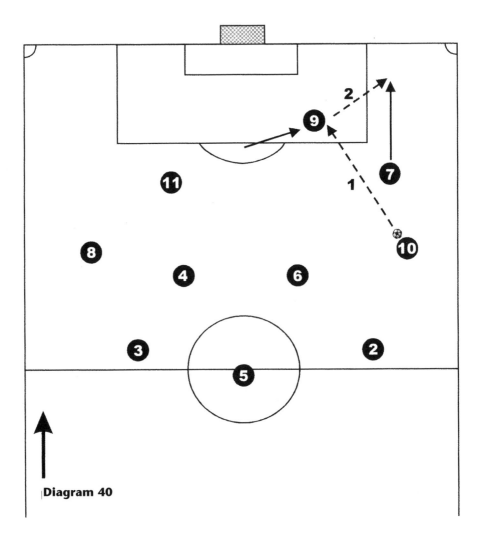

Diagram 40

Pass from the wing to the side midfielder who is penetrating (diagram 41)

Side back 2 makes a deep pass to wing 7, who makes a wall pass for the deep penetration of side midfielder 10. Side midfielder 10 then crosses.

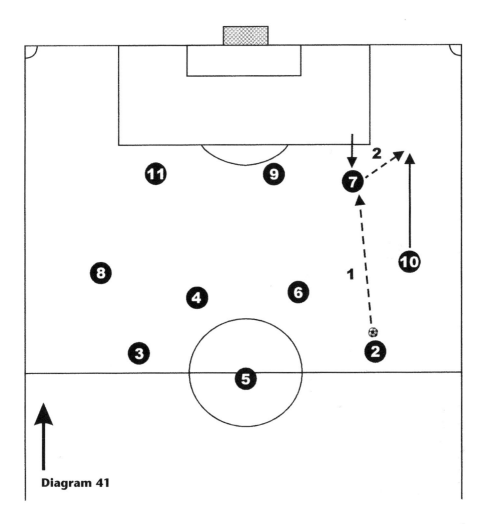

Diagram 41

"Pass and go": from the side midfielder to the wing (diagram 42)
Side midfielder 10 makes a one-two pass with the wing, then crosses.

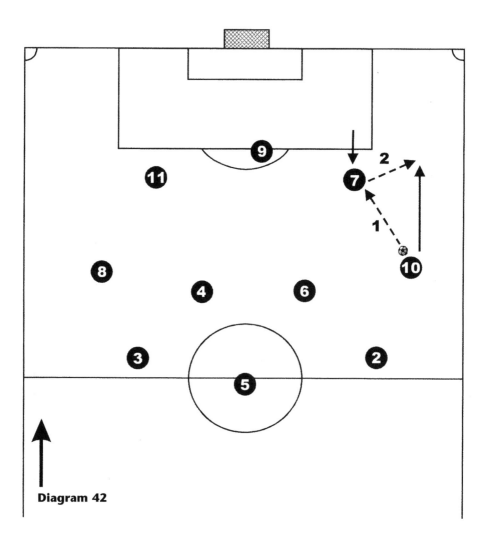

Diagram 42

Dummy movement by the wing to favor the side midfielder (diagram 43)
Center midfielder 6 passes to 7, who makes a dummy movement to support the deep penetration of side midfielder 10, who then crosses.

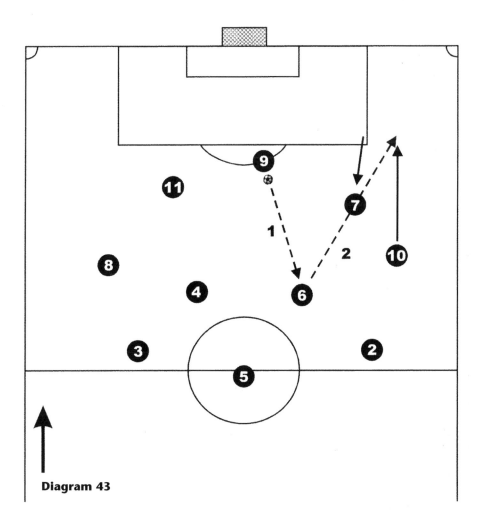

Diagram 43

Dummy movement by the wing to favor the side midfielder (diagram 44)

Center midfielder 6 passes to 11, who makes a dummy movement to support the deep penetration of side midfielder 8, who then crosses.

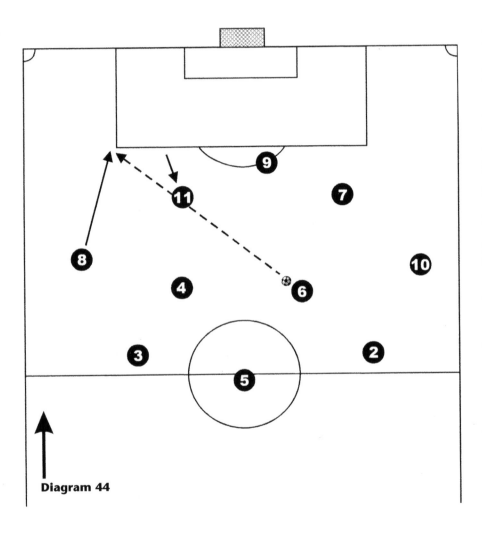

Diagram 44

Pass from the wing to the overlapping side midfielder (diagram 45)
Wing 7 supports the penetration by side midfielder 10 who carries out an overlapping movement and then crosses.

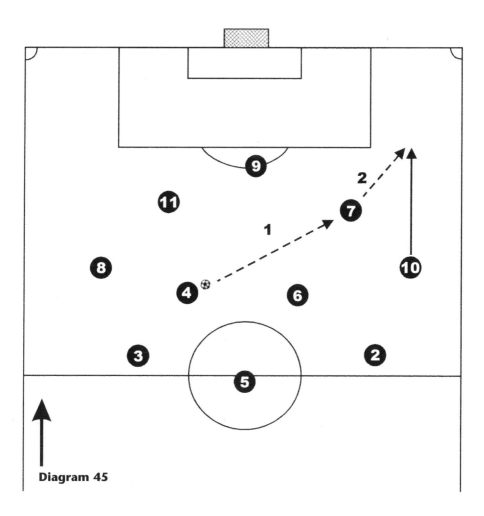

Diagram 45

CHAPTER THREE
DEFENSIVE SCHEMES

Tasks of the players according to their position:
- **Central back:** he must cover the side back and switch the marking on the opponent when the side back covers in diagonal defense.
- **Side back:** he must cover the side midfielder or mark one of the opposing forwards, trying to anticipate his actions.
- **Side midfielder:** he must become the fourth back on the weak side of the field.
- **Center midfielder:** he counters the opposing central back when the latter moves forward with the ball.
- **Wing:** he becomes the fourth midfielder on the weak side of the field.
- **Center-forward:** he must force the opponents' play towards the wings.

Double-teaming:
- **The side midfielder** double-teams the opponent with the ball being marked by the side back.
- **The center midfielder** moves backward and double-teams the opponent with the ball in the central part of the field.
- **The wing** moves backward and double-teams the opponent being marked by the side midfielder.

Covering:
- **The center midfielder** covers the wing or the side midfielder upfield.
- **The side** back covers the side midfielder downfield.
- **The central back** covers the side back.

Preparatory phase (diagram 46)

The team gets ready for the defensive phase by "getting compact", so as to close down the spaces and shorten the time available for the opponents to make a play.

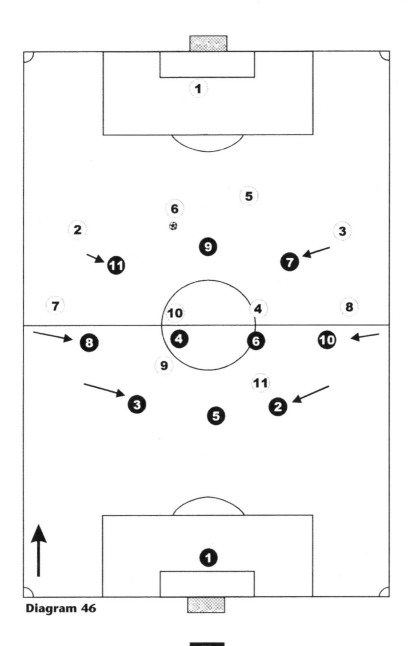

Diagram 46

Forcing (diagrams 47 and 48)

The defense's first objective is to force the opponents to develop their play towards one side of the field, so as to create a "weak" and a "strong" side. In diagram 47, the center-forward forces opponent 6 to develop the play on one side.

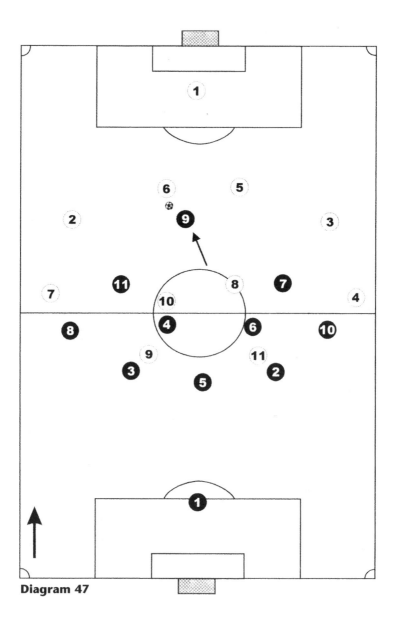

Diagram 47

If the opponents try to develop their play along the center of the field, for example by making a pass to a central back who moves forward, then the central back can be tackled by center midfielder 6. On the weak side of the field, wing 11 moves backward thus supporting the midfield, while left side midfielder 8 becomes the fourth back. The objective of center midfielder 6 is to force the opponents to develop their action on the side.

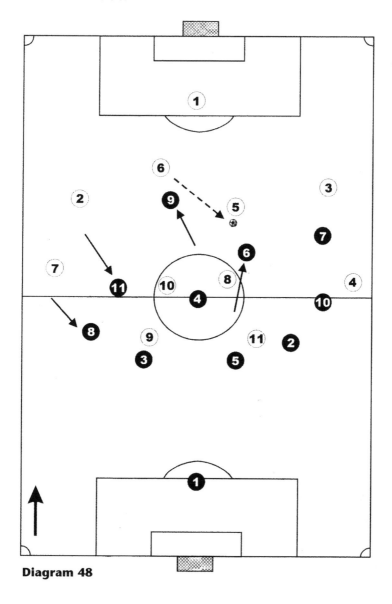

Diagram 48

Interception (diagrams 49, 50, and 51)

Once the opponents have moved their action to one side, wing 11 applies pressure on the opponent with the ball, while his midfield teammates shift towards the zone of the ball and his teammates on the opposite side (wing 7 and side midfielder 10) move backward and integrate with the midfield section (wing 7) and with the defense section (side midfielder 10). In this way, the defense becomes a four-player defense.

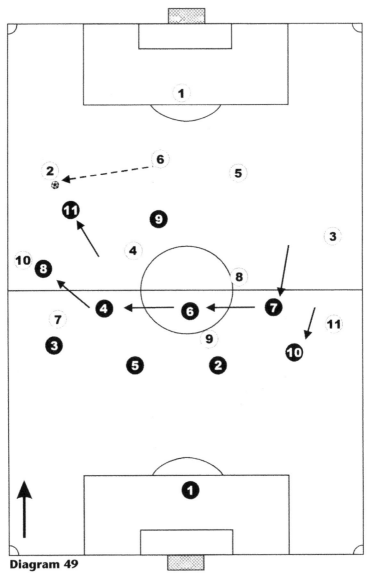

Diagram 49

When applying pressure, wing 11 tries to force the opponent to play to the side, where his teammate (side midfielder 8) will try to anticipate his direct opponent. Side midfielder 8 is covered by center midfielder 4, who is ready to intercept a possible diagonal pass towards the center and is covered by side back 3.

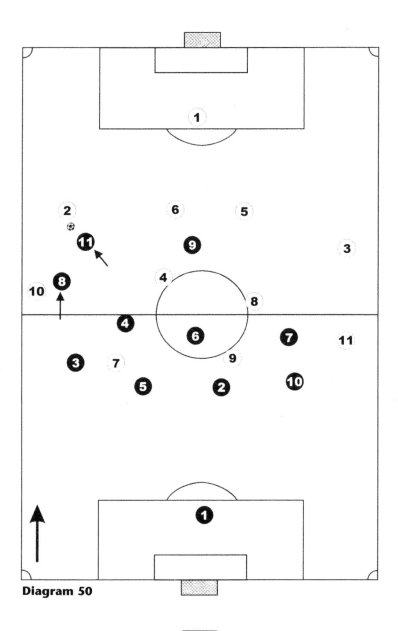

Diagram 50

If side midfielder 8 cannot anticipate the opponent, he applies pressure while waiting for wing 11 to double-team.

If the opponent manages to dribble the ball past 8 and 11 then, if the opponent moves forward along the sideline, the covering players who must tackle him are center midfielder 4 or side back 3.

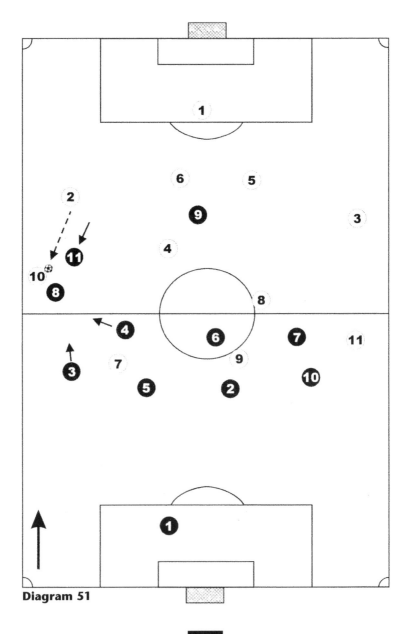

Diagram 51

Adjustment (diagram 52)
This shows how the team adjusts if the opponent receives the ball or dribbles it past the midfielders. Side back 3 faces the opponent while being very careful not to let the opponent dribble the ball past him. In this way the offense does not gain superiority in numbers and side midfielder 8 will have time to move backward and double-team.

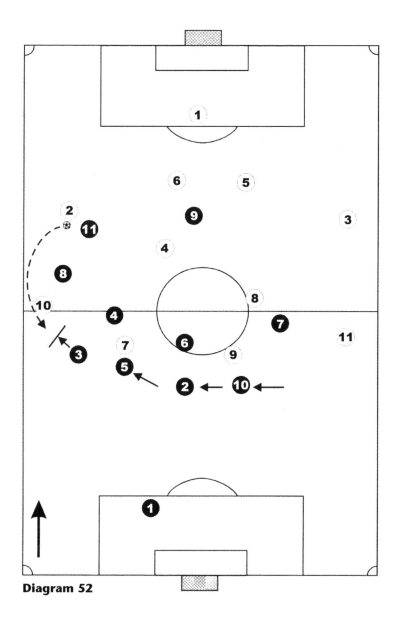

Diagram 52

Forcing on the center midfielder (diagram 53)

If opponent 2 makes a pass to opponent 4, then center midfielder 4 applies pressure on opponent 4 while his teammates arrange a diagonal defense according to the principles of zone play. Center midfielder 4 must force the opponents to develop their play on one side, while being very careful not to let the opponent dribble the ball past him.

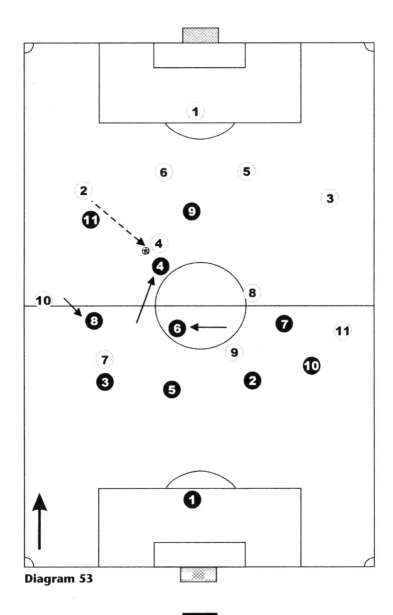

Diagram 53

Interception (diagram 54)

If the opponents switch the play to the opposite side, then wing 7 moves forward to apply pressure. Left side midfielder 10, who had momentarily become a member of the defensive line, moves forward to intercept a possible forward pass or touch while all the other teammates move towards the zone of the ball. Wing 7 must try to support the interception by his teammate 10 by forcing the opponent to play along the sideline.

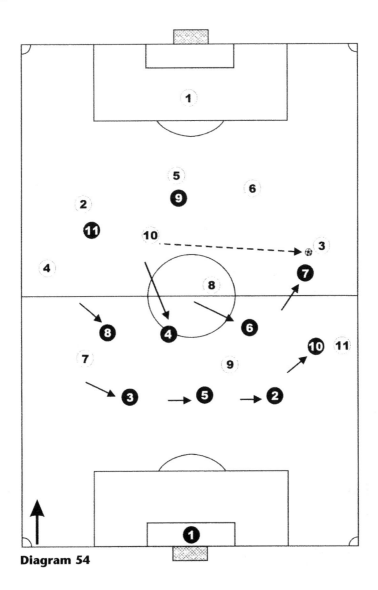

Diagram 54

Forcing and long pass (diagram 55)

When center-forward 9 applies pressure to force the opponents' play, they may opt for a long pass to the forwards.

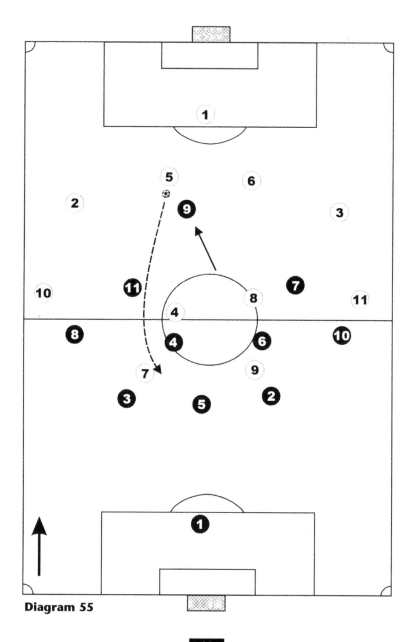

Diagram 55

Interception of the long pass (diagram 56)

The opponent who receives the ball is tackled by side back 3, who tries to anticipate him while being covered by his teammate, central back 5, who moves back a few yards to give him this coverage support. The center midfielder who is closer to the action (4) double-teams and all the other players move back, taking up an active position. The two side midfielders (8 and 10) integrate the defensive line, while the two wings (11 and 7) integrate the midfield.

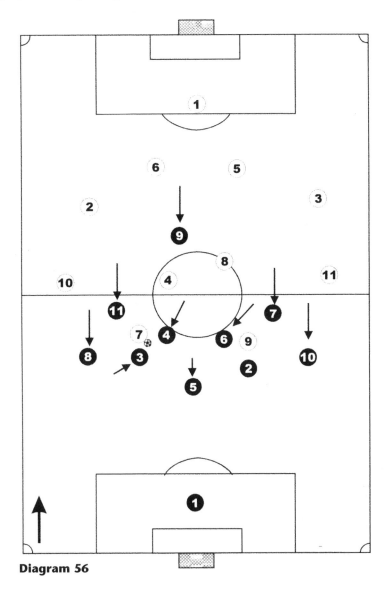

Diagram 56

Adjustment (diagram 57)

Diagrams 57 and 58 show how to adjust the team when the opponents build their action with a pass along the side to a forward.

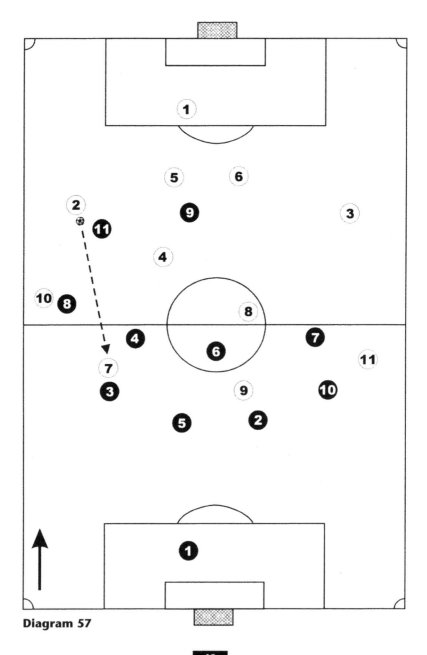

Diagram 57

Interception (diagram 58)

If the opposing forward receives the ball with a pass along the side, the side back (3) tackles him while the midfielder who is closer to the action (4) double-teams him. Central back 5 covers the side back and the other players move diagonally backward towards the zone of the ball.

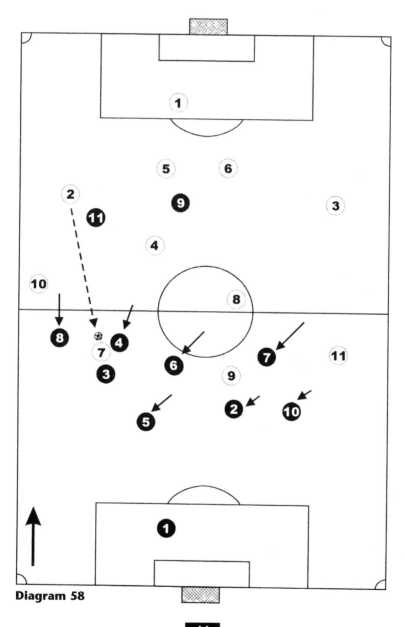

Diagram 58

CHAPTER FOUR
METHODS AND EXERCISES

- The coaching method.
- Exercises for the defensive phase.
- Exercises for the offensive phase.

The coaching method

As shown in diagram 59, the exercises are divided into three kinds.

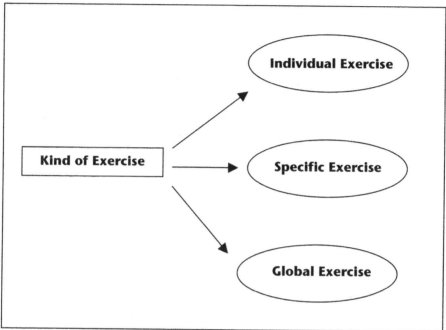

Diagram 59

Individual exercises are carried out by either the individual player or by players in pairs. They are meant to convey to the players basic tactical knowledge and to define the relationship between two players who play close to each other.

Specific exercises involve a whole section (the defense, the midfield or the attack). Their objective is to emphasize the tactical tasks of the players of the same section and the integrations occurring in two neighboring sections.

Global exercises involve two sections or the whole team, and simulate situations in team play.

Other exercises are aimed at coaching a single phase (offensive or defensive), and also multiple phases. The multi-phase exercises, involving small sided games, require the players to be involved in all the phases of the game (offensive and defensive) in a continuous alternation.

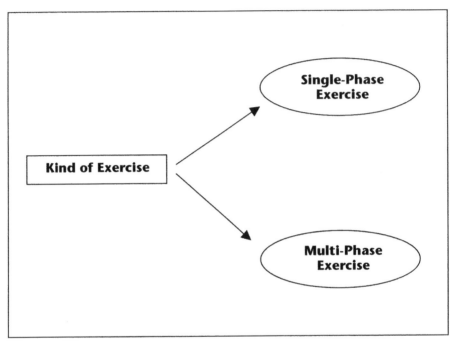

Diagram 60

The first step of our recommended coaching method is to start with single-phase individual exercises. This enables the individual player to learn basic tactical principles.

The second step is to use single-phase specific exercises in order to "build" the teamwork of the different sections.

The third step is to use multi-phase specific exercises, in order to coach the sections of the team to switch offensive and defensive phases in a continuous way.

The fourth step is to coach the whole team through specific single-phase global exercises.

Finally, multi-phase global exercises are used to simulate regular situations of play.

Exercises for the defensive phase

Single-phase individual exercises:

1. The defender is in a 20 x 10-yard rectangle and must tackle the forward who has the ball and is trying to dribble it past him. The objective of this exercise is to coach individual defending skills and technique (position, technique and timing of the tackle). See diagram 61.

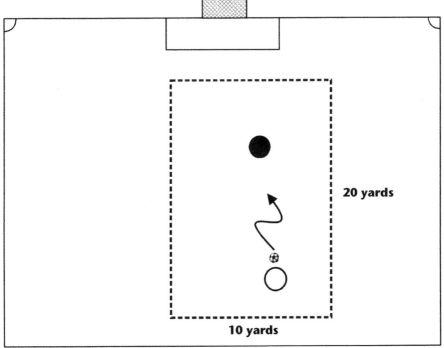

Diagram 61: one on one

2. The defender is inside the square shown in diagram 62. He must tackle two forwards who are passing the ball to each other trying to reach an advantageous position from which to shoot. The objective of this exercise to improve the defender's ability to buy time for the defense to react and support and to force the play of the opponents.

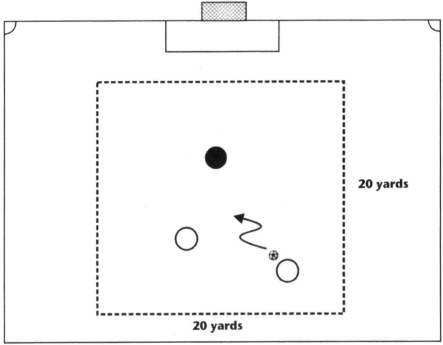

20 yards

20 yards

Diagram 62: one defender against two opponents.

3. Two defenders must tackle three forwards who are passing the ball to one another trying to score a goal. The objective of this exercise is to coach both the skills seen in the previous pages (technique, timing of the tackle, forcing) and the tactical relationship between two defensive players. Their main task will be to force the ball to one side, thereby creating a strong and a weak side. Special consideration should be given to the correct positioning of the defender who is farther from the ball, as he will have a twofold task: to be ready to intercept the pass and to cover his teammate. When it is impossible for the defender to take a position that enables him to perform these two tasks at the same time, then being ready to intercept the ball should take priority over covering.

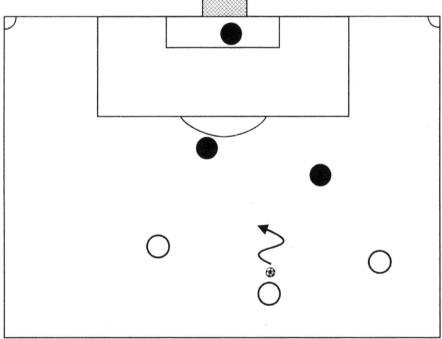

Diagram 63: two defenders against three opponents.

Single-phase specific exercises:

4. The defense section is arranged with the three players along the same line. The three defenders must take up the appropriate positions with regard to the three forwards, while the midfielders pass the ball to one another (see diagram 64). Later, the forwards will be involved too and so the defenders, in addition to taking up the correct positions with regard to their opponents, will have to cover the defender who has moved forward to tackle the ball (see diagram 65). In this exercise, the only task of the offensive players is to circulate the ball, so that the defense section can learn the correct positions and distances. After arranging the offense in a 3+3 pattern, the situation can be changed by moving a forward back to the midfield line, so as to form a 4+2 pattern.

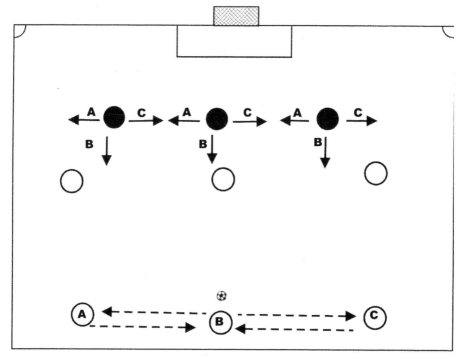

Diagram 64: Coaching the correct distances.

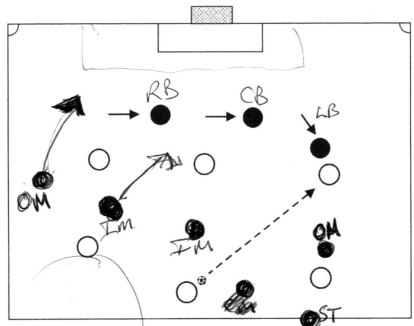

Diagram 65: Coaching the correct distances, covering and shifting.

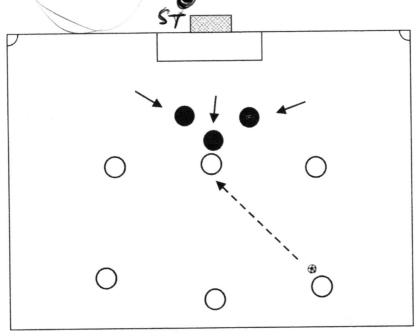

Diagram 65B: Coaching the correct distances, covering and shifting.

5. In the fifth exercise, the sections are arranged as in the previous one. The difference is that now the forwards, besides passing the ball to each other, are instructed to also try to dribble it past the defender and to carry out combinations. Besides teaching the players the correct positioning and distances, the objective of this exercise is to coach them to cover, to recover their position and, by shifting, to react appropriately to situations of inferiority in numbers.

6. This exercise gets the players used to shifting. Three defenders and a goalkeeper face four (or five) forwards, whose objective is to score a goal (see diagram 66).

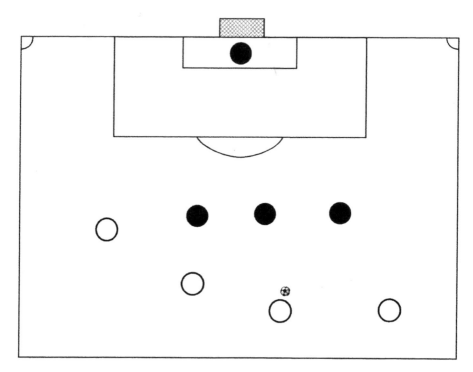

Diagram 66: Three defenders against four (or five) opponents.

Single-phase global exercises:

7. The objective of this exercise is to compact the midfield section and the defense section. The seven players of the two sections must attack seven silhouettes (or seven small flags or seven passive players) arranged as in diagram 67. The coach calls out on which silhouette (or small flag or opponent) the defensive players must attack and apply pressure. The objective of this exercise is to integrate and synchronize the movements of the midfield and defense sections. The side midfielders move backward on the weak side of the field, the midfielders double-team with the near back, and the backs anticipate their opponent when the near side midfielder applies pressure on another opponent (see diagrams 68 and 69).

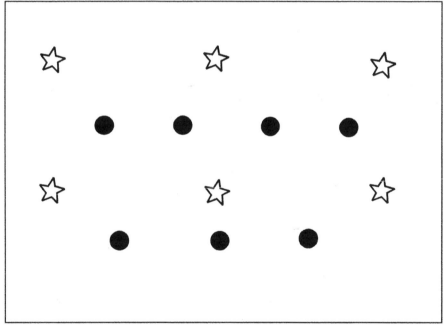

Diagram 67: Starting position.

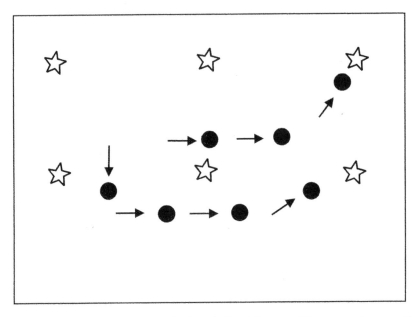

Diagram 68: The players attack the right side top silhouette (or small flag or opponent), and the left side midfielder moves backward to integrate with the defense section.

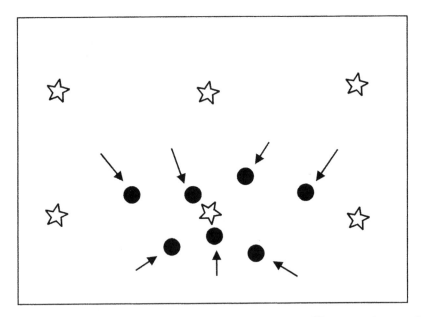

Diagram 69: The players attack the center bottom silhouette (or small flag or opponent), and the midfielder double-teams.

8. The seven players (plus the goalkeeper) play against ten opponents (arranged according to a 4-4-2 or 4-3-3 or 3-4-3 pattern). The opponents are active and try to score a goal. The task of the seven players belonging to the midfield and to the defense sections is only to intercept the ball. This is a single-phase exercise.

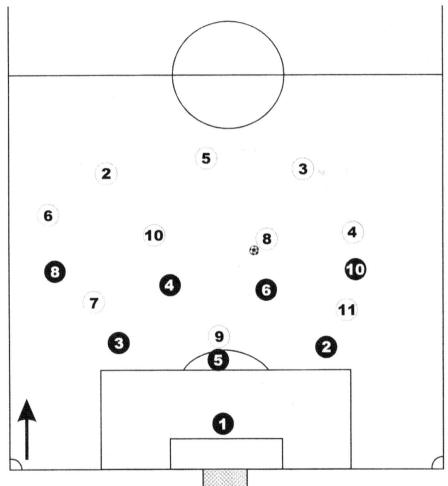

Diagram 70: Seven against ten.

9. The objective of this exercise is to compact the midfield section and the offensive section. The seven players of these two sections are guided by the coach to move forward and tackle the opponent, as in the exercise carried out by the defense and midfield sections. See diagrams 71 and 71B below.

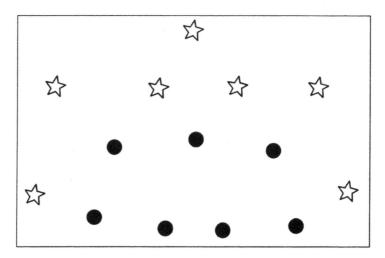

Diagram 71: Four defensive midfielders and three defensive forwards: starting position.

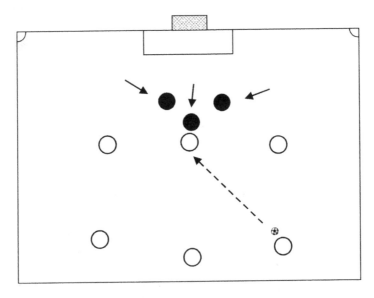

Diagram 71B: The four midfielders and the three forwards move forward and attack the silhouettes (or small flags or opponents).

10. In this exercise, the seven players play against 8 opponents (plus the goalkeeper) whose objective is to take the ball with their feet beyond a line 10 yards past the midfield line (diagram 72).

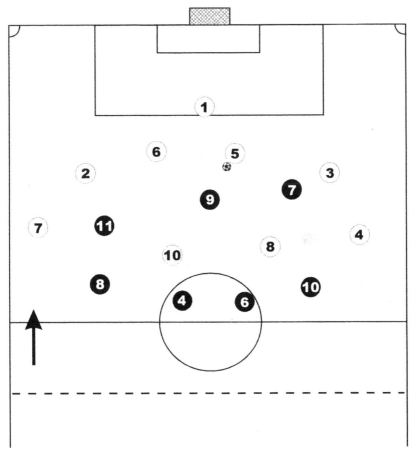

Diagram 72: Seven against eight.

11. Finally, the whole team is involved in simulating a defensive exercise against 11 passive players who pass the ball to one another with their hands. The coach must make sure that the horizontal and vertical distances, both among the players within the defense and within the offense, and also between the offensive and defensive units, is correct. In this exercise it is important to check the way players double-team, cover and integrate with the sections by

shifting forward or backward, and recover to an active position, after the opponent has taken the ball past them (see diagram 73).

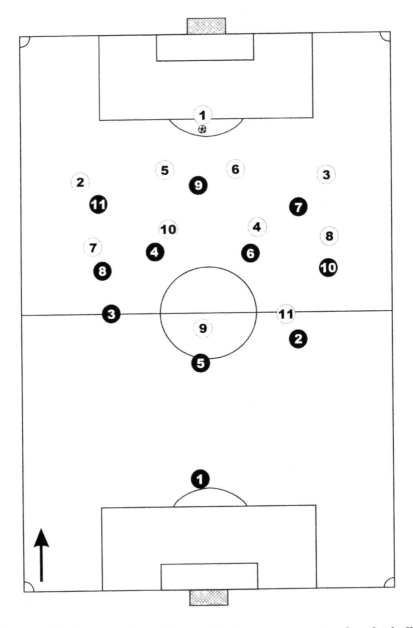

Diagram 73: Eleven against eleven match: the opponents play the ball with their hands.

12. After coaching the team by simulating a match (or "shadow" match) the players can play the following single-phase small sided match:
    Eight (3-4-1) plus the goalkeeper, against ten.
    Nine (3-4-2) plus the goalkeeper, against ten.
    Finally, eleven against eleven only in the defensive phase.

Multi-phase global exercise:

13. The last exercise in this coaching plan is the regular match, eleven against eleven.

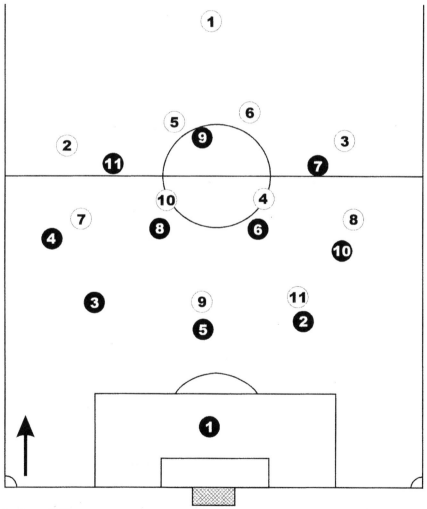

Diagram 73B

Exercises for the offensive phase

Single-phase individual exercises:

1. Three forwards must take the ball past two opponents and score a goal. In this three on two situation within the zone shown in diagram 74, the coach should assess and correct each forward's tactical choices. During the action, the forward must be able to optimize his positioning (by unmarking himself) and when he has the ball he must elect between dribbling the ball forward or passing it, choosing the time and the best technique.

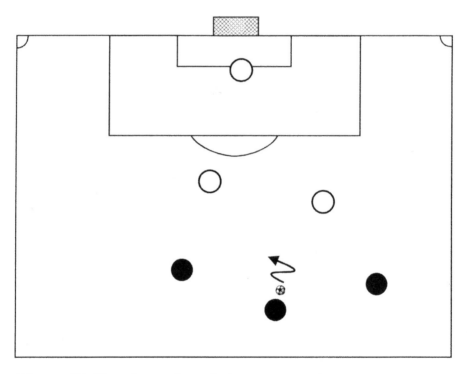

Diagram 74: Three forwards against two opponents.

Single-phase specific exercises:

2. The three backs and the goalkeeper play a simulated game with the objective of getting the backs used to passing the ball to one another. The goalkeeper starts the exercise by passing the ball to one of the three backs, who starts the building-up phase of the offense with the help of the other backs. The coach should carefully check the movement of the side backs, who should move horizontally towards the sides or towards the center, according to

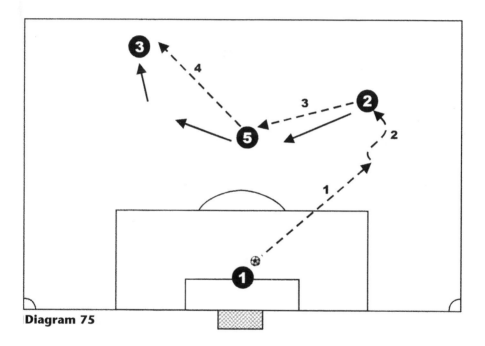

Diagram 75

the position of the ball. The central back must always be ready to support his teammate with the ball. Diagram 75 shows the correct movement of left side back 3: he goes towards the side when the ball is passed to the central back by right side back 2. When central back 5 passes to left side back 3, right side back 2 covers by moving towards the center. It is important that central back 5 supports the side back with the ball by making himself available for a possible back pass. This exercise gets the backs used to moving forward slowly, with either side back dribbling the ball forward for a short distance and then, either on his own initiative or at the coach's signal, turning and passing the ball to the central back who, in turn, immediately passes to the other side back who has moved towards the side. The side back receives, dribbles the ball forward for a short distance on the opposite side, then makes a back pass to the central back who is supporting him.

3. After the game simulation exercise, three backs plus a goalkeeper play against two opponents. The backs must take the ball beyond the midfield line, as shown in diagram 76.

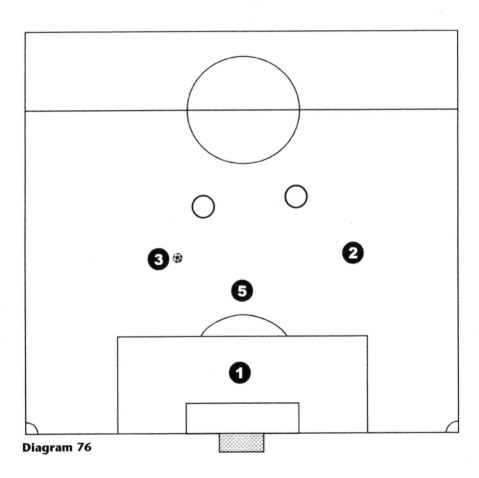

Diagram 76

4. After the backs, the four midfielders carry out the same exercise (described at point 2 above). See diagram 77.

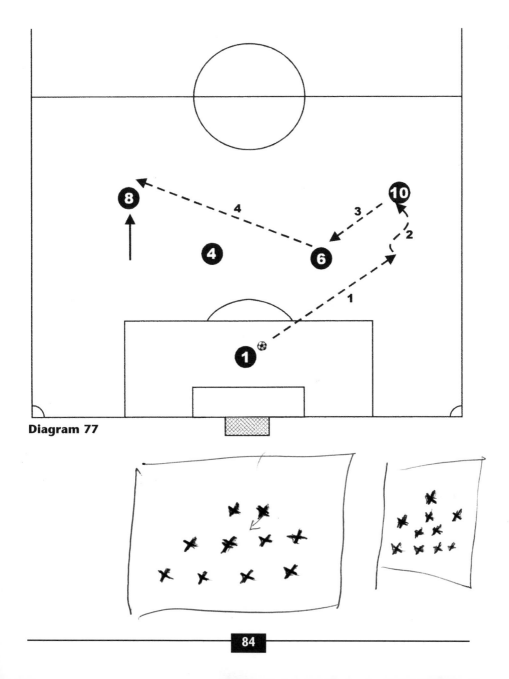

Diagram 77

5. After carrying out the exercise described in point 2 above, the four midfielders are asked to take the ball beyond the midfield line while being tackled by three opponents (diagram 78).

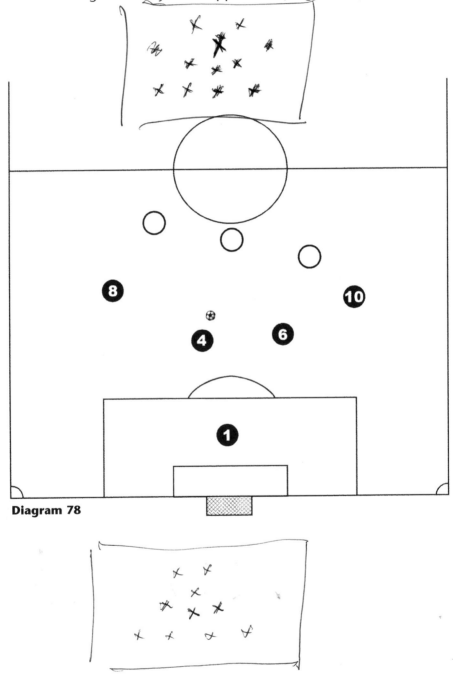

Diagram 78

6. After coaching the backs and the midfielders, it is now the forwards' turn. The forwards are asked to take the ball beyond the midfield line after carrying out one of the following final touches:

➤ Wall pass by the center-forward for the wing.

➤ Penetrating pass from the wing to the center-forward or for the far wing cutting in.

➤ Combinations between the wing and the center-forward.

The coach starts the scheme, by choosing one after another the player to whom to pass the ball (diagram 79).

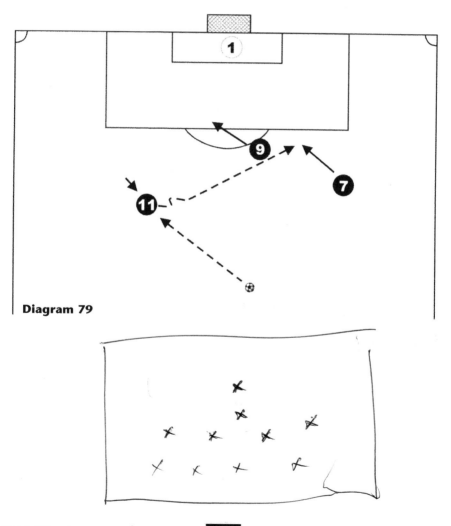

Diagram 79

Single-phase global exercises:

7. After coaching each of the three sections separately, a good exercise to build up an offensive subphase involves the backs together with the midfielders. The objective of these seven players is to take the ball beyond the midfield line while being tackled by five opponents. The coach should assess each player's tactical choices and should require a smooth development of the action of his players (see diagram 80).

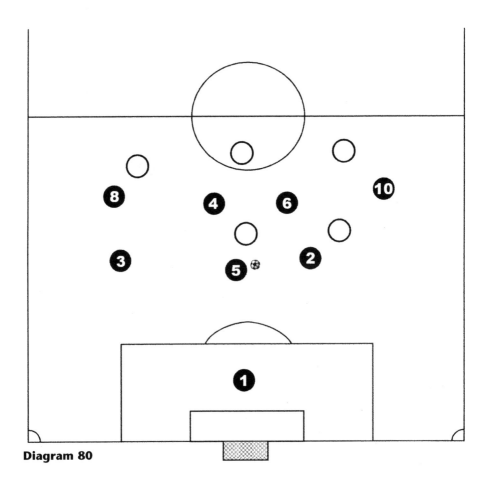

Diagram 80

8. The "attack" is then added to the two sections involved in the previous exercise, so that the whole team is now arranged on the field. The objective of the team is to pass the ball to one of the center midfielders through a volley back pass by a forward. This exercise is fundamental for the next phase, which is the final touch. When the midfielder receives the ball he is facing the goal, so the position is ideal for a penetrating pass or a diagonal pass to the opposite side of the field. The exercise starts with a "shadow" match, i.e. without any opponent tackling the team. Then, an increasing number of active opponents is arranged on the field (diagram 81 shows 11 against 6).

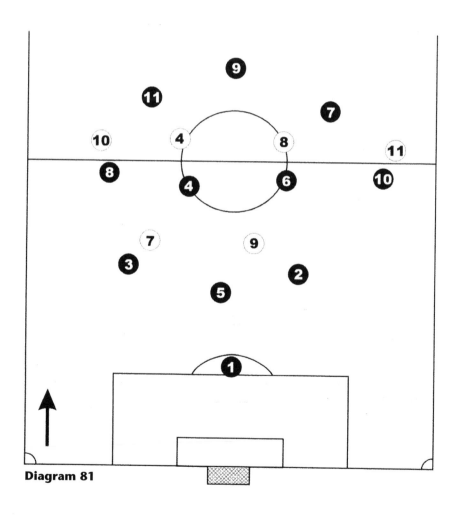

Diagram 81

9. To coach "final touches" and "shots on goal", the three sections are required to build up and finalize the action according to the schemes ordered by the coach. In ordering the schemes, the coach must take into account the skills of the available players. This exercise is carried out without opponents so as to help the players concentrate on and maximize the speed of performance (diagram 82).

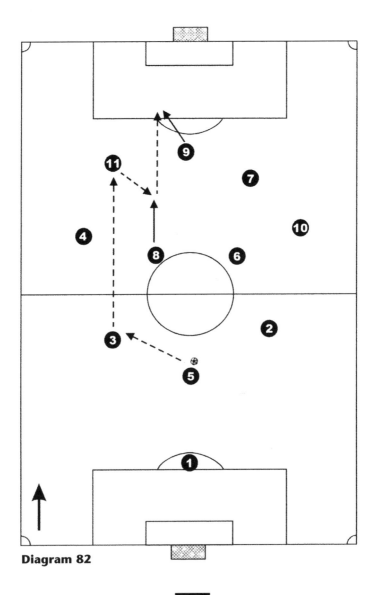

Diagram 82

Single-phase global exercises:

10. This is an important exercise to make the team quickly shift from defense to offense. While eleven players are simulating a defensive phase (without opponents and without the ball), the coach throws a ball to one of the players. The player who receives the ball must immediately start an attack with his teammates to give his team an opportunity to shoot by applying one of the schemes learned.

11. The typical multi-phase coaching exercise is the friendly match. If the opposing team we play is in an inferior division to ours, then the match is especially a test for the offense. On the contrary, if the opposing team is in a superior division to ours, then the match becomes an important test for the defense.

3-4-3

CONCLUSION

The concepts we have outlined are not and cannot be considered as absolute truths. Instead, they are ideas to stimulate discussion and investigation of our opinions.

This book has specifically dealt with the 3-4-3 pattern of play, but I think it is fundamental, even if self-evident, to make it clear that no guaranteed successful winning pattern of play exists, nor is it possible.

The idea of writing a book analyzing the opportunities provided especially on offense by the application of the 3-4-3 pattern of play, comes from the belief that in soccer, as in all fields of life, building is more important than destroying.

By analyzing the way in which the Italian "serie A" teams are arranged on the field, we can see how varied and valuable is the range of patterns.

This variety is a positive factor for soccer, as it challenges every coach and team to face other coaches and teams who apply similar or different ideas. This continuous challenge is a fundamental factor in the tactical evolution of soccer.

Massimo Lucchesi

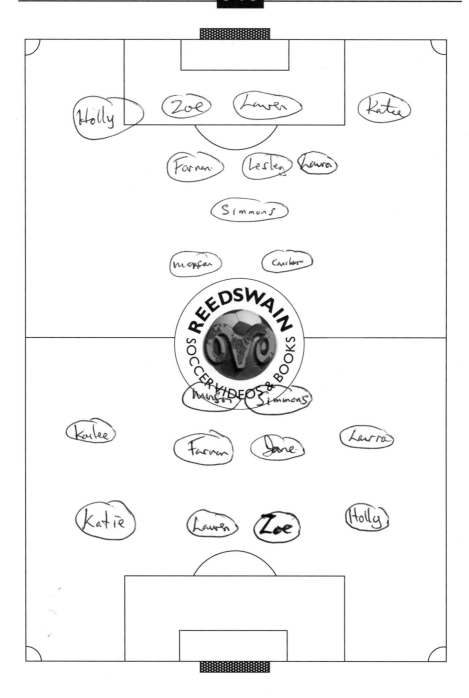

REEDSWAIN BOOKS

#291 Soccer Fitness Training
by Enrico Arcelli and Ferretto Ferretti
$12.95

#169 Coaching Advanced Soccer Players
by Richard Bate
$12.95

#225 The Sweeper
by Richard Bate
$9.95

#256 The Creative Dribbler
by Peter Schreiner
$14.95

#788 ZONE PLAY
A Technical and Tactical Handbook
Angelo Pereni and Michele Di Cesare
$14.95

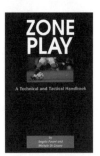

#793 Coaching the 5-3-2 with a Sweeper
by Fascetti and Scaia
$14.95

#794 248 Drills for Attacking Soccer
by Allessandro Del Freo
$14.95

#167 Soccer Training Games, Drills and Fitness Practices
by Malcolm Cook
$14.95

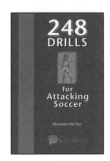

#267 Developing Soccer Players THE DUTCH WAY
by Kormelink and Seeverens
$12.95

765 Attacking Schemes and Training Exercises
by Fascetti and Scaia
$14.95

1-800-331-5191 • www.reedswain.com

REEDSWAIN BOOKS

#254   101 Youth Soccer Drills
Ages 7-11
by Malcolm Cook
$14.95

8
+ 2
10

#255   101 Youth Soccer Drills
Ages 12-16
by Malcolm Cook
$14.95

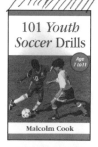
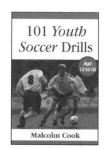

#785 Complete Book of Soccer Restart
Plays
by Mario Bonfanti and Angelo Pereni
$14.95

#261 Match Analysis and Game
Preparation
by Kormelink and Seeverens
$12.95

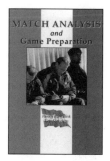

#262 Psychology of Soccer
by Massimo Cabrini
$12.95

#264 Coaching 6 to 10 Year Olds
by Giuliano Rusca
$14.95

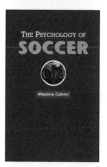
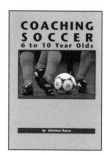

#792 120 Competitive Games
and Exercises for Soccer
by Nicola Pica
$14.95

#905 Soccer Strategies:
Defensive and Attacking Tactics
by Robyn Jones
$12.95

#816 Playing Out of Your Mind
A Soccer Player and Coach's Guide to
Developing Mental Toughness
by Alan Goldberg
$9.95

1-800-331-5191 • www.reedswain.com

#154 Coaching Soccer
by Bert van Lingen
$14.95

#185 Conditioning for Soccer
by Raymond Verheijen
$19.95

#177 Principles of Brazilian Soccer
by Jose' Thadeu Goncalves
$16.95

**#175 The Coaching Philosophies of
Louis van Gaal and the Ajax Coaches**
by Kormelink and Seeverens
$14.95

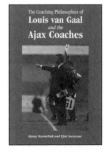

#244 Coaching the 4-4-2
by Marziali and Mora
$14.95

#789 Soccer Scouting Guide
by Joe Bertuzzi
$12.95

**#264 Coaching Soccer
6 to 10 year Olds**
by Giuliano Rusca
$14.95

#284 The Dutch Coaching Notebook
$14.95

#287 Team Building
by Kormelink and Seeverens
$9.95

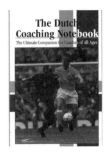

#786 Soccer Nutrition
by Enrico Arcelli
$10.95

612 Pughtown Road
Spring City PA 19475
1.800.331.519 • www.reedswain.com